Norman Lock

THE HOUSE OF
CORRECTION

BROADWAY PLAY PUBL

357 W 20th St., NY NY 10011
212 627-1055

THE HOUSE OF CORRECTION

Copyright 1988 by Norman Lock

First Printing: October 1988
ISBN: 0-88145-061-8

Design by Marie Donovan
Word processing: WordMarc Composer Plus. Postscript typographic controls: Xerox Ventura Publisher. Output in Palatino at 1270 dpi: Linotronic 300.
Printed on acid-free paper and bound by BookCrafters Inc., Chelsea MI

This play is for Helen, Dorothy, and George, and with it the author acknowledges with gratitude and affection his debt to his first friends in the theatre, Kip Gould and Bradford O'Neil, and to his mother and father.

ABOUT THE AUTHOR

Norman Lock is also the author of WATER MUSIC, which was produced at The Perry Street Theatre in New York in 1983; FAVORITE SPORTS OF THE MARTYRS, which was premiered by The Changing Scene in Denver in 1987; and two new plays, LEAD BABY and IN THE OCCUPIED TERRITORIES. In addition, he has published poetry and short fiction in literary reviews and magazines. He was awarded the Aga Kahn Prize for Fiction for the best short story published by *The Paris Review* in 1979. He is a member of The Dramatists Guild.

ORIGINAL PRODUCTIONS

THE HOUSE OF CORRECTION premiered at New Playwrights Theatre, Ashland, Oregon, on April 9, 1987, with the following cast:

STEVE . . . . Peter Kjenaas
MARION . . . . Katie King
CARL . . . . Michael Pocaro

Bradford O'Neil directed and designed this production. Virginia Ruffulo was the Stage Manager.

THE HOUSE OF CORRECTION was subsequently produced by The Los Angeles Theatre Center, Bill Bushnell, Artistic Producing Director, and Diane White, Producer. It opened on January 15, 1988, with the following cast:

STEVE . . . . Christopher McDonald
MARION . . . . Katie King
CARL . . . . Ron Campbell

Bradford O'Neil directed this production. Douglas D. Smith designed the set and lighting; Jon Gottlieb, the sound. Sherry Linnell created the costumes. Nancy Ann Adler was the Stage Manager.

CHARACTERS

MARION, middle 30's. She is just beginning to get heavy, but it is a heaviness that can still be mistaken for voluptuousness.

STEVE, early 30's. Intelligent and obsessed. In his obsession with justice (correction), he may even be brilliant. Certainly his theories on the whole psychological/parapsychological rigmarole are brilliantly conceived, if bizarre.

CARL, middle to late 30's. MARION's husband. Writes award-winning ad copy for the New Jersey Asparagus Council. His path leads from bourgeois complacency through terror to bourgeois emasculation. In the end, he has learned nothing.

Time: The present. Summer. Thursday evening to Sunday night. One year later.

Setting: CARL and MARION's house in a "pleasant bedroom community starting in the upper 70's," over the bridge in New Jersey. The action takes place in the living room, basement workshop, master bedroom, and kitchen. Other than essential furniture (sofa and chair, workbench and "electric chair," double bed, kitchen set), stage requirements are minimal.

ACT ONE

Scene 1

(The living room. Thursday evening. Summer. The present.)

(Darkness)

(Laughter, in the darkness, a man's and a woman's. It builds slowly to something very near hysteria.)

(Suddenly, lights up. STEVE and MARION are sitting on the sofa, drinking coffee, and looking through a photo album.)

(After a moment, CARL enters from street. He is dressed in a business suit and carries a briefcase. He has just arrived home from his job in the city. He lives over the bridge in New Jersey. It is dinner time.)

CARL: I'm home.

MARION: Hello, dear. Look who's here.

STEVE: *(Waving from the sofa)* Hi, Carl.

CARL: *(Warmly)* How are you?

STEVE: Hot.

CARL: It's the weather.

MARION: I've been bringing Steve up to date. Showing him pictures of our trip to the islands.

CARL: *(Sitting)* Oh, fine, fine.

STEVE: It looks like a nice trip.

CARL: It was.

STEVE: The hotel—

CARL: Four star.

MARION: *(To* STEVE*)* More coffee?

STEVE: Please.

(She pours him coffee.)

STEVE: The room had a view?

CARL: A beautiful view of the ocean.

MARION: It was lovely. There was a cage of little birds in the room. Little tropical love birds.

STEVE: Do any sailing?

CARL: Oh, sure. We sailed every morning and laid around the beach all afternoon.

MARION: The ocean was the most wonderful blue. I've never seen anything like it.

STEVE: I'll bet it was nice.

MARION: It was. It was so nice. I wish you could have been there. In fact, not a day went by when I didn't say to Carl: "Wouldn't Steve love this?" Not an hour.

CARL: That's true. We missed you. You would have made the whole trip complete.

STEVE: It's nice of you to say so.

CARL: We mean it. Don't we, Marion?

MARION: Of course. And the ocean was so lovely, so...

STEVE: Blue?

MARION: The bluest blue I've ever seen!

(Pause)

CARL: Indigo.

STEVE: Pardon?

CARL: Indigo. I believe that's the color that best describes it.

STEVE: You have an artist's eye.

CARL: Well, I do have a set of watercolors.

STEVE: You paint—I didn't know that.

CARL: Not really—not exactly paint.

MARION: Oh, Steve, Carl does the loveliest watercolors.

STEVE: I'll bet he does. I'll bet he just paints up a storm.

CARL: Dabble is more like it. I dabble in watercolors.

MARION: He does the loveliest sailboats.

STEVE: Does he?

MARION: They're quite accomplished.

STEVE: I'd love to see them.

MARION: They're upstairs. In the master bedroom.

STEVE: Oh.

MARION: Sailboats. With white sails on blue—

STEVE: Indigo.

MARION: Indigo water. Bays, lakes...whole oceans! With the sun setting. He does sunsets over water remarkably well.

CARL: There's a trick to it. You just make these little broken red lines in the water.

MARION: And once in a while there's a lighthouse.

STEVE: A lighthouse!

CARL: They're impressionistic.

STEVE: I'd love to see them.

MARION: They're upstairs—

STEVE: In the master bedroom.

MARION: Right.

STEVE: Maybe later?

MARION: *(Acknowledging the innuendo)* We'll see.

CARL: You're staying for supper—aren't you, Steve?

MARION: Yes, do stay! We're having your favorite.

STEVE: Well, seeing that you're having my favorite...

MARION: Good!

CARL: Afterwards, we'll talk over old times, with the help of a snifter of Napoleon.

MARION: We have a lot to talk about.

STEVE: Yes, we do.

MARION: Years and years.

STEVE: Of course I can see life's been good to you.

MARION: We've done all right—haven't we, Carl?

CARL: We've been lucky. Touch wood.

MARION: Carl's done amazingly well since he left the Civil Service.

STEVE: Your home is very nice.

CARL: All Marion's doing. She's the decorator in the family. I have absolutely no sense of design.

MARION: That's not true, Carl. You have a good eye for things. For colors. Every time I see one of your sailboats I say to myself: "Carl missed his calling." You could have been an artist, dear. But, of course, you are an artist. With words. *(To* STEVE*)* A brilliant wordsmith, that's what he is.

CARL: I'm not brilliant—

MARION: Oh, yes you are! Everybody says so. *(To* STEVE*)* Last year Carl won a Clio for the brilliant work he did for the Asparagus Council of New Jersey.

STEVE: Clio?

MARION: A very important prize. He was honored for his advertising copy.

CARL: *(With the air of one launching a joke)* I have to admit my work for the Asparagus Council was fresh.

(He and MARION *laugh.)*

MARION: It was brilliant!

CARL: *(Seriously)* Yes, it may have been brilliant. At least it verged on...brilliance. It made my agency career really take off.

MARION: Like a rocket! He just goes up and up. We're all so proud of him. Last year we finally saw our way clear to own a home of our own. Yes. Our own home.

CARL: It's lucky you knew where to find us, Steve.

STEVE: It wasn't too difficult. I asked around.

CARL: Ah.

MARION: Everyone knows Carl.

CARL: Now don't exaggerate, Marion.

MARION: It's true. You are very well known in this town.

CARL: I have been spreading myself around lately.

STEVE: What do you mean?

CARL: Getting myself known. It's important to make friends in the business and outside the business. You never know.

STEVE: No, you don't.

MARION: If we did, wouldn't we be lucky?

STEVE: But you have been lucky.

MARION: Oh, of course. We're doing very nicely, thank you.

CARL: And what about you, Steve? How have you been?

STEVE: Not so lucky.

CARL: Oh, really? I'm sorry to hear that.

MARION: So am I.

STEVE: My wife was brutally murdered.

MARION: How awful for you.

CARL: That must have hit you pretty hard.

STEVE: I went out of my mind.

MARION: Truly out of your mind?

STEVE: Truly. Right out of it. For weeks.

MARION: I've never met anyone who went out of their mind. Not even for an hour, much less weeks! Did you, Carl?

CARL: No. At least not in civilian life. I did see a guy in the Army go out of his mind. He began to beat his head against the wall. I'll bet he must have beaten his head against the wall twenty-five times before he finally passed out.

MARION: That many! I wouldn't have thought you could beat your head against a wall that many times and live.

CARL: It was quite a thing to see.

STEVE: Didn't you try and stop him?

CARL: Stop him? No...I didn't know him that well.

MARION: *(To CARL)* What made him go out of his mind?

CARL: He wanted to go home.

MARION: Is that all?

CARL: Apparently.

MARION: Well, that doesn't seem a good enough reason to beat your head against a wall.

CARL: No.

STEVE: *(Softly)* I tore my house apart.

MARION: Was this while you were out of your mind?

STEVE: That's right. I went on a rampage.

MARION: I've never met anyone who went on a rampage either.

STEVE: You've been lucky like you said.

CARL: You went on a rampage because your wife died?

STEVE: Murdered. My wife was murdered.

MARION: Brutally, you said. Don't you remember, Carl? He said she was brutally murdered. And that's what made him go out of his mind. Right, Steve?

STEVE: Right.

MARION: What happened then?

STEVE: Then?

MARION: After you tore apart your house.

STEVE: It was only an apartment really. We never did manage to get a home of our own.

MARION: It took us years and years. *(To* CARL*)* Didn't it, dear?

CARL: That's right. We had to struggle.

MARION: We scrimped and saved—it seemed like forever.

CARL: We built a life founded on work, mutual trust, and love.

MARION: Lots of love!

STEVE: *(Violently)* Will you shut up!

MARION: *(Taken aback)* Oh!

CARL: *(Overlapping)* Now look...

STEVE: You stupid...!

CARL: *(Firmly but fairly)* Now look, Steve—just because we're old friends, we don't have to take that.

MARION: We certainly don't! Especially in our own house! Our castle. Am I right, Carl?

CARL: Absolutely.

STEVE: *(Anguished)* I'm trying to tell you about my wife!

MARION: The one who died—we remember. We were listening. But really, Steve, just because you have had a personal tragedy doesn't give you the right to be rude.

CARL: This is our house, Steve. And in our house we do not raise our voices, we do not lose our temper. The world outside can shout and stamp its feet and go to pieces, but here, in this house, we are calm. Rational. We are in control of ourselves.

STEVE: *(Quietly)* I am grieving.

CARL: Of course you are. You have had a major upset in your life. We sympathize. Believe me, our hearts bleed for you. We, too, have lost people near and dear to us. Mothers, fathers...assorted relations. Thank God not a spouse! Not yet! We are no strangers to grief. But grief should be dignified. You must master it not let it master you. Going out of your mind for weeks...! Rampaging...destroying your apartment! I'll bet they asked you to leave, didn't they? Did they ask you to leave, Steve?

STEVE: Yes.

CARL: Of course they did. You destroyed their property. And I'll bet they kept your security deposit, too. I would have. If a tenant had destroyed one of my apartments, I would have kept his deposit and put him right out on the street. It's only fair. And I've thought about this, Steve—this is something I've thought about. Because I'm seriously considering getting into real estate. We've talked about it—haven't we, Marion?

MARION: Yes, we have.

CARL: You probably think I'm a hard-hearted bastard, don't you? Go on. Say it. I'm a hard-hearted bastard.

STEVE: You're a hard-hearted bastard.

CARL: I knew you'd say that, but it's all right. We're friends, and you have had a terrible thing happen to you. We understand.

MARION: We understand completely.

CARL: And we commiserate. Our hearts go out to you. Really, Steve, we are not without a social conscience. Not without pity for life's unfortunates.

STEVE: Victims.

CARL: Them, too. We donate old clothes, even money, for the victims of natural disasters at home and abroad. We write letters to local, state, and federal governments demanding aid for the sick and the needy. Right in this house, upstairs at my desk, on an old Smith Corona manual typewriter I picked up at a yard sale, I have written the president! Over the years, letter after letter, I have pounded away till my fingers ached on behalf of those less fortunate than myself.

MARION: Think of the stamps, Steve!

CARL: That's right, and as the price of a first-class stamp went up and up over the years, there was never a corresponding decrease in my letter-writing. It made no difference. Good God, we're Democrats! We've always been Democrats! To hell with the deficit—people come first. The people must be considered. And I think you'll agree, Steve, that these are not the words of a hard-hearted bastard. We wish we could do more—we'd love to do more.

MARION: We'd love to!

CARL: I wish we had the room. We'd invite all the homeless in New York City to come and stay with us. But obviously this is not possible. There isn't room. We couldn't afford to feed them all.

MARION: And they carry diseases and things.

CARL: So you see, Steve, we are not in a position to open our doors however wide our hearts may be open. We are not a social service agency.

STEVE: What about me?

CARL: You? What about you?

STEVE: I'm homeless. I've got no place to go. I don't know where I'm going to sleep tonight.

CARL: Why don't you find yourself another place to live? There is no shortage of apartments in town.

STEVE: I have no money.

CARL: Save it. Life isn't easy. You must learn thrift.

STEVE: I lost my job.

CARL: Lost your job? How?

STEVE: I went to the office drunk. I tore apart the filing cabinets. I threw the water cooler out a fifteenth story window. I roughed up the typing pool. I was dismissed on the spot.

CARL: We abhor violence.

STEVE: I was out of my mind.

CARL: With grief, we know. But really, Steve, we expected a whole lot better of you. Upsetting the office routine...roughing up women!

MARION: *(To* STEVE*)* What exactly did you do to them? The women, I mean.

CARL: It's irrelevant what he did to the women! He should never have laid a hand on them.

MARION: I just, you know, was curious about what he did to the women.

CARL: I forbid you to be curious on the subject of sex. It's not something nice people think about in the daytime. We aren't a couple of prurient teenagers looking up dirty words in the unabridged.

STEVE: Vagina.

MARION: *(Shocked)* Oh!

CARL: *(Overlapping)* I beg your pardon?

STEVE: Cunnilingus.

MARION: Cunna what?

CARL: Shut up, Marion!

STEVE: Soixante-neuf.

CARL: That's better.

MARION: *(Ingenuously)* I love to hear French spoken. It's so romantic.

CARL: Now look, Steve...we don't appreciate that sort of talk in our living room. We're a decent married couple. I can't stress that enough.

STEVE: Sorry. It's because I'm nearly out of my mind with sorrow.

CARL: Nearly! *(Laughs)* I'd hate to see you when you're totally out of it.

STEVE: I tear things apart.

CARL: So you've said. *(Worried)* Tell me...You don't feel—there's no chance of that happening now, is there?

(Pause)

STEVE: No, I'm in control.

CARL: That's good, because if there was any chance of your going on the rampage here, I'd have to ask you—as one old friend to another — to leave. There are a great many valuable things here, antiques and such, that I'd hate to see smashed.

STEVE: I'm O.K.

CARL: I'm counting on you, Steve.

STEVE: *(Violently)* I'm O.K.!

MARION: He says he's O.K., Carl, and I think we should give him the benefit of the doubt. He is a friend of the family.

CARL: That's just what I'm willing to do...give him the benefit of the doubt. It's what I always do. You know why, Steve?

STEVE: No, why?

CARL: Because I'm a liberal. I consider it my responsibility to give the guy under me every break. Let him prove himself and rise—I'll make room for him. It's a big world, and I don't begrudge anybody success.

STEVE: So what about it?

CARL: What about what?

STEVE: Can I move in with you until I'm on my feet again?

CARL: *(Slightly shocked)* In here? With us?

STEVE: Just until I find another job.

CARL: I don't know, Steve...

MARION: Oh, I think we should.

CARL: *(Surprised)* You do?

MARION: Yes. We should hold out a helping hand to this poor, suffering individual and invite him under our roof.

CARL: *(Doubtfully)* Our actual roof? You're sure you're not speaking metaphorically?

MARION: I'm sure. Let's offer Steve our protection. We have a spare bedroom...guest towels. It's what friends are for.

(Pause)

CARL: All right. We'll do it! That's what friends are for!

(He holds out his hand to STEVE.*)*

STEVE: *(Taking* CARL's *hand)* Thank you, Carl. Thank you, Marion. I appreciate it. I'll just step outside a minute and get my suitcase. Give you a chance to talk privately.

CARL: What is there to talk about? It's all settled.

STEVE: I'll be right back then.

(Exits)

(Pause)

CARL: It's a wonderful thing you're doing, Marion.

MARION: You'd do the same for one of my friends.

CARL: What do you mean one of your friends? Isn't he a friend of yours?

MARION: I've never seen him before in my life.

(Blackout)

Scene 2

(The basement workshop. The following evening.)

(Lights up. STEVE is making something. Whatever it is, it's too early to tell.)

(After a moment, CARL enters.)

CARL: So here you are.

STEVE: Here I am.

CARL: Marion said you were down here.

STEVE: You've got a nice little shop.

CARL: Yeah, though I'm hopeless when it comes to tools and things.

STEVE: Then why have it?

CARL: I don't know...It's one of those things you just have—if you have a basement. Sometimes I like to come down here and just look at all the screwdrivers and saws. I like to drive a nail once in a while. It relaxes me.

STEVE: My old man did home remodeling for a living. I used to help him sometimes. I'm pretty good with my hands.

CARL: What's that you're making?

STEVE: Can't tell yet.

CARL: Just messing around, hunh?

STEVE: That's right. Just messing around. Who knows...It may turn into something. *(Pause)* Something on your mind?

CARL: No.

STEVE: Liar.

CARL: What?

STEVE: I said you're a liar.

CARL: Now look...Who do you think you are? *(Pause)* As a matter of fact, there is something I want to talk to you about.

STEVE: See? I was right.

CARL: I don't want you to think me rude or inconsiderate after all you've been through...

STEVE: Thank you.

CARL: You're welcome. But my wife and I were wondering... We were wondering who you are.

STEVE: A friend of the family, remember?

CARL: No—

STEVE: I'm not a friend of the family?

CARL: The fact is neither of us have ever laid eyes on you before last night.

STEVE: So that's what's bothering you.

CARL: I wouldn't say it was bothering me...

STEVE: You wouldn't?

CARL: Not exactly...

STEVE: Not exactly, but it is, shall we say, upsetting you?

CARL: Well, yeah, I think that's a fair way of putting it.

STEVE: That you're upset.

CARL: Yes. Both Marion and I are upset. You're a complete stranger for God's sake!

STEVE: Oh, is that all?

CARL: Isn't that enough? You're in our guest room under false pretenses.

STEVE: How do you mean "false pretenses"?

CARL: We—that is, Marion and me—each assumed that the other one knew you. That you were a friend...of Marion's...or mine. You understand?

STEVE: Did I ever say I knew either one of you?

CARL: No, at least not to me, but you were on the sofa together when I got home. She introduced you as...as if you were a long lost friend.

STEVE: You jumped to conclusions, didn't you?

CARL: Goddamn it, we both did! And you knew it and said—did nothing to set us straight. And that's upset me.

STEVE: Perhaps she wanted you to think we were old friends.

CARL: Why would she do that?

STEVE: So that you'd invite me to move in.

CARL: (Angrily) What are you suggesting?

STEVE: Nothing.

CARL: We are very happy, and you are here only because of my generosity.

STEVE: I said I'm not suggesting anything.

CARL: You better not be. My wife and I are happy!

STEVE: Are you?

CARL: Yes. Very happy. We are in a position now...to be... happy. After fourteen years. We can be happy. As happy as we want. So we don't want any outside influences spoiling our happiness.

STEVE: (Quietly) She needs someone to jump her bones.

CARL: What did you say?

STEVE: Nothing.

(Pause)

CARL: You're a very strange man, Steve.

STEVE: She needs a good fucking.

CARL: I heard that! Look, I'm going to have to ask you to leave.

STEVE: Sorry.

CARL: No, really. You can't get away with saying things like that. I can forgive a lot, knowing that your tragedy has probably unhinged you...

STEVE: What tragedy?

CARL: Your wife's death.

STEVE: Ah, that.

CARL: Well, yes, of course that! I don't think you're yourself, Steve.

STEVE: You're probably right.

CARL: It's understandable. I mean Marion and me both understand that a man whose wife—let me put it this way...When violence—horror suddenly comes out of nowhere into your life—abruptly, like it did yours...there's bound to be upset, confusion. You're going to talk and act peculiarly for a while.

STEVE: That's a very compassionate attitude.

CARL: Compassion—yes! That's the great thing in a case like this, and that's why we want you to know...we understand and are willing to forgive...much and...

STEVE: And?

CARL: And—but you know, Steve, we don't know who you are.

STEVE: Yes, I know.

CARL: And even ignoring the fact that you are under our roof under false colors—

STEVE: Colors? What colors are those, Carl?

CARL: Please let me finish! You are here because of a mistake. But it was ours—I'm willing to give you the benefit of the doubt and accept full responsibility for your being here.

STEVE: That interests me very much, Carl.

(He takes out a pocket notebook and pencil and begins to take notes.)

CARL: What does?

STEVE: That you're willing to accept responsibility.

CARL: For your being here, yes.

STEVE: For my being here—I've been waiting to hear you say that.

CARL: (Surprised) You have?

STEVE: Yes. I want you to be and to feel responsible.

CARL: Well, I've always been aware—acutely—of my responsibility to my fellow beings.

STEVE: Even animals?

CARL: I'm a member of the zoo. I wrote letters to the auto companies protesting head injury experiments on live baboons. What are you writing?

STEVE: Just taking a few notes. So you're opposed to suffering?

CARL: That's right. Suffering offends me. It makes me feel sick inside and hurts my sense of...

STEVE: Your sense of design?

CARL: No, what a strange thing to say! My sense of what's right.

STEVE: You consider suffering unseemly.

CARL: I didn't say that! Look, I'm having trouble putting this into words.

STEVE: But you're a wordsmith! You won a fucking Clio for your brilliant work in asparagus.

CARL: Advertising, Steve...That was advertising. This on the other hand is something else again.

STEVE: This is an area where you cannot lie.

CARL: I told you before I do not lie! Neither in the spoken word or the written word. In my copy I am absolutely truthful.

STEVE: Absolutely?

CARL: One hundred percent. *(Slight pause)* As far as I know.

STEVE: Define as far as you know.

CARL: Well, I'm only a copywriter after all, not a technical person. I take what the technical people give me and dress it up. I make it flow.

STEVE: But suppose they—the technical people—aren't telling you the truth?

CARL: I'm sure they are.

STEVE: How can you be?

CARL: Because I deal with honorable people.

STEVE: How do you know?

CARL: This isn't the nineteenth century! I'm not selling snake oil in the backwoods!

STEVE: Aren't you?

CARL: The whole philosophy of business—I'm talking about legitimate business—is different. Business is no longer out to hoodwink the consumer. Instead, we try to educate him to the benefits of the product.

STEVE: And if the product is bad?

CARL: There are no bad products anymore.

STEVE: I see. And you, as a responsible man, make it your business to investigate every product before you dress it up in award-winning words?

CARL: That's not necessary. Nor is it possible. I take what they tell me on trust.

STEVE: Trusting in their honorable intentions toward the public?

CARL: That's right.

STEVE: That's very interesting, Carl.

(He closes the notebook and returns it to his pocket.)

STEVE: I wondered how it happened.

CARL: How what happened?

STEVE: How it works. It's very interesting. I'm glad you told me. Now let me ask you one last question. What—just supposing now—what if, by some unaccountable fluke, a product which you have helped to sell to the consumer—you, Carl, as the advertising copywriter—suppose the product turned out to be bad, even harmful. Are you willing to be responsible?

CARL: *(Considering)* Well, supposing—and it's only a supposition—if people bought a harmful product because of my words... I could not be held accountable, no. If the facts were misrepresented by the manufacturer, or not known by them at the time, I could not be held...responsible.

STEVE: But would you feel responsible?

CARL: Feel?

STEVE: If, say, someone got sick, seriously ill, or was maimed because of your words. Would you feel responsible for his or her suffering?

CARL: No. I cannot accept that. I simply take what they tell me and make it lively—that's all I do. Do you understand what I'm saying?

STEVE: I understand.

CARL: That's not to say I wouldn't feel sorry...

STEVE: Of course.

CARL: Now, Steve, what I came down to talk to you about is just how long do you intend to remain here with us? We're perfectly willing to put you up, temporarily; but in all fairness to Marion, I think we should set some sort of time limit—don't you agree?

STEVE: I agree.

CARL: Good. Then shall we say Sunday? Sunday night? That gives you three days to get yourself situated.

STEVE: Sunday night will be fine.

CARL: That's O.K. then. Thank you, Steve, for being so reasonable.

STEVE: Thank you, Carl.

(CARL *turns to go.*)

STEVE: Carl, I enjoyed your watercolors.

(Pause)

CARL: Oh? When did you see them?

STEVE: This afternoon while you were at work. Marion showed them to me. In the master bedroom. It's a very nice bedroom.

(Pause)

CARL: You were in the bedroom with Marion?

STEVE: Yes. It's a lovely bedroom. My wife and I weren't lucky enough to have such a bedroom, with so many lovely things. *(Slight pause)* Such a soft mattress.

CARL: You tried the mattress?

STEVE: I really must compliment you on your watercolors. They're exquisite.

CARL: Where was Marion while you were looking at them?

STEVE: And I really must compliment you on your wife.

CARL: How do you mean?

STEVE: She has such nice skin. Really exquisite.

CARL: What are you trying to say? What happened in the bedroom? *(Slight pause)* Did anything happen in the bedroom between you and Marion?

STEVE: She was so nice to me. Her skin is so clear and pink and pretty.

CARL: *(Screams)* No!

STEVE: Yes, Carl. And she squealed just like a pink little piggy. She was so happy. We both want her to be happy. Marion's happiness is everything.

CARL: You're lying!

STEVE: I'm not the one who lies, Carl.

CARL: You're a fucking liar!

STEVE: What kind of language is that? In this house such language is forbidden. In this house such language is unseemly.

CARL: I'll kill you!

(He goes for STEVE, but is easily subdued. STEVE immobilizes him by pushing one arm up behind his back.)

STEVE: The world may shout and stamp its feet, but here in this house we will have peace and decency. We will stay in control of ourselves.

CARL: You're hurting me!

STEVE: Are you suffering, Carl?

CARL: You're breaking my arm!

STEVE: The bedroom paper is very chic. It is indigo with a pattern of tiny roses and green fern...

CARL: *(Like an animal)* Awww...!

STEVE: The bedspread is elegant. A pale green to match the pale green of the ferns.

CARL: Bitch!

STEVE: And the sheets are rose-colored satin. Cool against the skin.

CARL: Whore!

STEVE: Her skin is soft...like rose petals, Carl. Like moss ...damp moss. I buried my face in it, and for a moment I was in heaven. Heaven! For a moment I forgot all my troubles.

(CARL *is quiet, exhausted by his struggle and his emotions.* STEVE *releases his arm, and he slumps onto the floor.*)

STEVE: I'm building something, Carl. Something which will make us all feel better. No, I can't tell you what it is yet. You're not ready. But you will be. And when you are, I'll show you. It won't take me long—I'm handy. I'm very good with my hands. Ask Marion, ask your lovely wife. Oh, it's no trouble, Carl, no trouble at all. It will be ready by Sunday night. Sunday night is our deadline. As an ad man you know all about deadlines. No, don't thank me. It's the least I can do for such a good friend.

(Blackout)

Scene 3

(The master bedroom. A few minutes later.)

(Lights up. MARION *is in bed, reading a magazine and eating an apple.)*

(After a moment, CARL *enters. He is angry and upset.)*

MARION: What's the matter, Carl? You look awful.

CARL: I want to know what happened between you and Steve today.

MARION: Well, let me see if I can remember. It was a long day. I made him french toast. I showed him the back yard. Then, I think, we talked about the pre-Socratic philosophers. He's marvelously well read. You'd enjoy talking to him.

CARL: Aren't you forgetting something?

MARION: I don't think so...Let me think.

(She thinks.)

MARION: No, I can't remember anything of significance.

CARL: Significance! You went to bed with him! Don't you consider that significant? I do. I call that damned significant.

MARION: *(Laughing easily)* Oh, that! I wondered what you were talking about. That was nothing, Carl, nothing at all.

CARL: Then you admit it? It's true? I hoped it wasn't true. Oh, Christ, Marion...How could you?

MARION: *(Lightly)* It was nothing—it meant nothing. I've already forgotten it.

CARL: *(Somewhat relieved)* Oh, well, that's different.

MARION: You see, silly? A meaningless encounter. I hardly knew it was happening.

CARL: Is that possible, Marion?

MARION: I thought of my mother.

CARL: But he said you squealed. He said you squealed just like a pink piggy.

MARION: *(Miffed)* Is that what Steve said? Well, I don't think that's very flattering! I'll have to talk to him about that. Pink piggy indeed!

CARL: Did you squeal?

MARION: Certainly I squealed! It hurt. It hurt and hurt.

CARL: But you didn't enjoy it? Not even a little bit?

MARION: Not even the teeniest bit.

CARL: That's all right then so long as it didn't give you any pleasure. He had me going for a moment, Steve did, downstairs in the basement.

MARION: What is he doing down there? He's been hammering all evening. It's getting on my nerves.

CARL: He's making something. He promised to show me Sunday night. *(Long pause)* Marion?

MARION: Hmmm?

CARL: Couldn't you have stopped him?

MARION: Oh, I don't think so. He's very forceful.

CARL: Yes. Sometimes I think he's just a little too forceful. It's irritating.

MARION: Steve can be irritating at times, but in the final analysis I think he's a fine man. I like him.

CARL: He scares me.

MARION: He's like a breath of fresh air.

(Pause)

CARL: Do you think we should call the police?

MARION: I wouldn't. We don't want to get him into trouble.

CARL: But he did threaten me. I believe he means to do me some harm.

MARION: Whatever for?

CARL: I don't know. But he was talking strangely just now, and he hurt me. He pushed my arm way up behind my back—like this.

(He demonstrates.)

CARL: I thought it would come right out of the socket.

MARION: I'm sure he didn't mean it. He was probably just playing. He's very playful.

CARL: I don't know...He said some terrible things.

MARION: Like what, Carl?

CARL: They don't bear repeating. And just what do we know about him? Nothing really.

MARION: I'm sure you don't have anything to worry about. And besides, it won't be for long.

CARL: I told him we were giving him until Sunday night. Then he would have to leave.

MARION: What did he say?

CARL: He thanked me.

MARION: There, what did I tell you? He's a fine man. You have nothing to worry about. Now come to bed.

CARL: All right.

(He strips to his shorts and gets into bed.)

CARL: He described it in detail.

MARION: What?

CARL: The wallpaper, the bed, the sheets. I didn't know we had satin sheets.

MARION: They're for special occasions.

(STEVE *enters suddenly. Throughout this scene, he prowls restlessly around the room. We sense the danger in him. If there is a dresser onstage, he rifles the drawers, emptying them onto the floor.*)

MARION: *(Startled)* Steve!

CARL: What do you want?

STEVE: I'm lonely all by myself.

MARION: *(To* CARL*)* Ah, he's lonely.

CARL: *(Angrily)* That's not my problem!

MARION: Carl! *(Whispering)* He's just lost his wife. Think how he must be feeling. Especially seeing us together, sharing the comforts—the delights—of the marriage bed.

CARL: *(Whispering)* What do you want me to do about it?

(They will continue to whisper together, calmly or furiously, until CARL *speaks to* STEVE.*)*

MARION: Make him feel welcome. For the few short days he will be under our roof, let's make him feel really welcome.

CARL: How much more welcome do you want him to feel?

MARION: If you're talking about what happened this afternoon — what could I do? It wasn't so much what he did, but what he said.

CARL: What did he say? *(Silence)* Marion, what did he say?

MARION: *(Shaking off her reverie)* Oh, nothing definite. He talked for a long time about things I didn't understand. The words were, you know, the same old words, but...

CARL: But what? Did he talk about painting?

MARION: No...not about painting...

CARL: What then?

MARION: He hinted.

CARL: Hinted? What kind of hints?

MARION: Hints may be too strong a word.

CARL: Half-hints then!

MARION: This may sound silly, but I got the impression that Steve is interested in our welfare.

CARL: He's probably on welfare, or some controlled substance.

MARION: *(Excited)* Do you sense that, too?

CARL: Sense what?

MARION: That he's on something—not one of those vulgar drugs you can buy on any street corner in New York, but something very special. There's something...visionary about Steve. Did you notice his eyes? They look like Jeffrey Hunter's, who played Jesus in *King of Kings* and came to a tragic end. Maybe it's not so much that he's *on* something as he's *onto* something.

CARL: But, Marion—

MARION: That's enough, Carl! There is something happening to us that's important to understand.

CARL: So what do you want me to do?

MARION: Invite him in.

CARL: In where?

MARION: Into bed with us.

CARL: I will not!

MARION: Unless you want me to lose all respect for you, you most certainly will!

CARL: But, Marion—he may be carrying some horrible disease. He may even have you-know-what. You know what the city is like. And the people who live and breathe right in the midst of it! People in apartment buildings with no real home of their own. They're dangerous! That's why those of us who can cross the bridge into New Jersey each night. It's our drawbridge, the river a moat around our castle. There's plague out there, Marion, and skin diseases and horror. The wind inside the city whistles like death.

MARION: Make room for Steve.

CARL: Is there no limit to our social responsibility?

MARION: Love thy neighbor—Christ's words, Carl—not mine.

CARL: I can't help thinking you're putting too strict an interpretation on that particular passage.

MARION: I believe that Steve has been sent to us by God.

CARL: You're not serious! What for?

MARION: To redeem us.

CARL: He's nothing like a Christ figure. Christ would never have biffed you.

MARION: He is the lost sheep, and God is waiting to see what we do with him.

CARL: I wish He'd sent us the lost spoon instead.

MARION: This is no time for irreverence. God is waiting.

CARL: Oh, all right! But just for tonight.

MARION: Wonderful! We're making progress.

CARL: It's hard.

MARION: Spiritual regeneration is never easy. But I think you'll agree the benefits of a quiet conscience and complacency are worth the trouble. Now go ahead and ask him, before he tears the room apart.

CARL: *(Still whispering)* Steve.

MARION: Louder.

CARL: *(In a normal voice)* Steve? Excuse me.

STEVE: Yes? What is it?

CARL: We were thinking you might like to sleep here tonight.

STEVE: In your bed?

CARL: That's right. We thought you'd be less...lonesome... here with us.

STEVE: That's nice of you, Carl.

CARL: So hop in.

(CARL *moves closer to* MARION. *Fully dressed,* STEVE *gets into bed next to* CARL.)

MARION: There. All nice and cozy. Isn't this lovely?

CARL: *(Petulantly)* Yeah.

STEVE: I don't like it.

MARION: Why not, Steve?

STEVE: I want to sleep next to you.

MARION: Ah...!

CARL: *(Overlapping)* Now just a minute!

MARION: What harm can it do? He misses his wife's warm body at night—isn't that so, Steve?

STEVE: That's so.

CARL: Why can't he be satisfied with my warm body?

MARION: *(Laughing)* Oh, Carl, you're so silly sometimes! You don't smell anything like a woman—does he, Steve?

STEVE: No, he doesn't.

CARL: What does that have to do with it?

MARION: If you don't know now, you never will.

CARL: I won't do it! You're pushing me too far.

MARION: I'm not sure I like your attitude.

CARL: I don't like your letting a complete stranger come between us in my own bed.

MARION: Shhh! *(Whispering)* How can you be so unfeeling?

STEVE: I want to sleep next to Marion.

CARL: Go to hell!

MARION: Now stop it, both of you! Why can't you be friends?

STEVE: I want to sleep next to Marion.

CARL: Shut your dirty mouth!

MARION: Move over Carl.

CARL: For Chrissakes, Marion—

MARION: MOVE YOUR ASS! NOW!

(CARL moves over. STEVE gets in between them.)

CARL: There, goddamn it! I hope you're satisfied!

(STEVE nestles next to MARION.)

STEVE: Thank you.

MARION: Such nice manners. It's a pleasure to have you in the same bed with us. *(Pause)* Your feet are cold!

STEVE: Sorry.

MARION: That's all right. They're not nearly as cold as Carl's. His are like ice. It's like they were dead.

(Pause)

(CARL has his back to them and is sulking. STEVE begins to fondle MARION under the covers. She squirms and giggles.)

MARION: Your hands are cold, too. Oh! Stop that, bad boy! Stop! *(Giggles)* Careful, you'll rip them! They're my best pair.

CARL: *(Sitting up)* Now that's enough! What's going on under there?

MARION: Nothing, nothing at all. Go to sleep, dear.

CARL: He's touching you—I know he is!

STEVE: So where's the harm in that?

CARL: You're not allowed to touch her!

STEVE: *(Laughing)* What quaint ideas you have! It's not like I'm causing her any pain.

CARL: According to everything that's holy, a wife is not allowed to accept another man's caresses while in bed with her husband.

MARION: It's my body, and I'll do what I want with it. What are you so upset about? I mean, really...What are we talking about? A hand. That's all. Five fingers doing things to me in the dark. With my eyes closed, they could be coming from anywhere. They could be spiritual in nature.

CARL: Bullshit! You don't expect me to believe you're getting felt up by Casper the Friendly Ghost?

MARION: It's only a hand. What's so terrible?

CARL: His hand!

MARION: And what's in a hand? Bones, muscle—nothing important. What I'm trying to say, Carl, is the hand is so far away from the brain and the heart that it has no more significance for me than an umbrella I might find on a bus. Or a...hat rack.

CARL: Hat rack! You think I'm stupid, don't you? Both of you.

STEVE: *(With quiet intensity)* Get out of the bed, Carl.

CARL: *(Exasperated)* I won't!

MARION: Never refuse a guest. That's a law of hospitality.

CARL: I will not get out of bed and leave my wife in the hands of a complete stranger.

MARION: *(Easily)* Steve and I are not strangers. He knows my body like a road map of one's home town.

CARL: Bullshit! Bullshit! Bullshit!

STEVE: *(Quietly)* Get out of the bed, Carl.

CARL: *(Savagely)* You fuck yourself!

MARION: I wouldn't make him mad if I were you. He has some terrible secret.

CARL: So what if he does?

MARION: Some terribly dark secret which makes him dangerous. Haven't you felt his danger? It makes me shiver.

STEVE: GET OUT OF THE BED!

(CARL leaps out of bed.)

MARION: *(Thrilling)* Oooo! I would be careful if I were you. With a man like that, things can happen—without warning. Violence. He can hurt you, Carl.

(CARL scuttles around to MARION's side of the bed.)

CARL: *(Pleading)* Come with me, Marion. If you love me, come with me.

MARION: *(Scandalized)* Where? It's the middle of the night! What would the neighbors think if they saw us running away from our own house in the middle of the night!

CARL: Please, he can have the house. *(To STEVE)* You can have the house and everything in it. The furnishings, the suits in my closet—my shoes if they fit! Take them. And there's plenty of food in the cupboards, in the refrigerator. The freezer in the basement is chock full of the best cuts of meat. It's all yours. I make you a present of the whole works. We'll never come back. Just let us have the car, and you can keep the rest. No one will bother you. When you run out of food, you can go next door. They have everything we have. Everything just the same. And after you finish with them, you can move on down the block. You never need want for anything.

STEVE: I won't have a wife.

CARL: But there are women all over! Women of every description. Married and unmarried. Widows. Girls. Virgins. You can have your pick. And many of them are beautiful. Not like Marion.

MARION: *(Indignantly)* I beg your pardon!

CARL: Marion's over the hill. She's thirty-four years old!

MARION: Thirty! I'll be thirty-one in eleven months. Don't let him trick you, Steve.

CARL: She has varicose veins—

MARION: I do not!

CARL: Cellulite. Bad breath. Her breasts have started to sag. She has two chins, and she's overweight. In a couple of years, she'll be fat as a house. You should see her mother!

MARION: All lies! Carl, you're such a dirty liar. I could never run away with a man who values me so little.

CARL: I need you, Marion! We'll go away right now, just the two of us. We'll start a new life. We'll drive all night up into Vermont or New Hampshire. We can start again.

MARION: It's too late.

CARL: It's not too late!

STEVE: *(Coldly)* I want Marion.

CARL: No! You're young and handsome. You can have anybody.

STEVE: But I want your wife.

MARION: *(Sighing)* It's a wonderful feeling—to be wanted.

CARL: But why her?

STEVE: Because she's yours.

CARL: I don't understand!

STEVE: You will. In time. In time everything will be clear.

CARL: *(At the end of his rope)* What's the big mystery?

STEVE: You must wait until the time is right.

CARL: When will that be?

STEVE: Soon. Sunday. You yourself set the deadline.

CARL: For you to leave!

STEVE: I like it here.

CARL: I want my house back. I want my bed back. And I want my wife!

STEVE: Are you feeling dispossessed?

CARL: Yes, that's exactly how I'm feeling.

STEVE: Good. That's how I want you to feel. Dispossession is the first step towards your purification.

CARL: I don't need purification.

MARION: He's right, Steve. He's very clean, very fastidious when it comes to personal hygiene.

STEVE: I'm not concerned with his personal hygiene. It's his soul that's at stake. His soul is corrupt, full of maggots. We must help him to cleanse it.

MARION: *(To* CARL*)* You see, he has your best interests at heart.

STEVE: *(To* CARL*)* And now it's time for you to go to bed.

CARL: Where? Do I curl up on the floor like a dog?

STEVE: You can have the guest room. The guest towels are hanging in the guest bathroom, waiting for you.

CARL: Guest!

STEVE: I'll see you at breakfast.

CARL: Come with me, Marion! *(Hopefully)* To the guest room?

MARION: *(Firmly)* I can't do that, Carl.

CARL: It's not far—a short way down the hall.

MARION: I'm sorry.

*(*STEVE *suddenly flicks open a switchblade and holds it at* MARION's *throat. She gasps.)*

STEVE: *(To* CARL*)* Does this help? Does this make it easier for you?

(It does make it easier for him.)

CARL: You won't hurt her?

STEVE: Not if you leave right now.

CARL: O.K. I'm going. Will you be all right, Marion?

MARION: I'll be fine.

CARL: I'll say goodnight then.

MARION: Goodnight.

STEVE: Goodnight. Oh, and Carl...Don't call the police. You won't, will you?

CARL: No, I won't.

STEVE: That's good. That's real good.

(Blackout)

Scene 4

(The kitchen. The next morning.)

(Lights up. MARION *is drinking coffee at the kitchen table.)*

(After a moment, CARL *enters. He hasn't slept and looks it.)*

MARION: *(Brightly)* Good morning, dear. Did you sleep well?

CARL: No.

MARION: I didn't think so. I could hear you moving around half the night.

CARL: I couldn't sleep.

MARION: What were you doing prowling around?

CARL: Thinking. *(Slight pause)* Do you know he's locked the basement door?

MARION: Really?

CARL: I couldn't get into the basement.

MARION: Why would you want to in the middle of the night?

CARL: To see what he's building! It has something to do with me. He said so.

MARION: Then why don't you just ask him what it is?

CARL: I did. He said I wasn't ready. What do you suppose he meant by that? I'm not ready...Ready for what? The whole situation is driving me crazy!

MARION: Relax...I've never seen you so wired. Have a drink, take a Darvon.

CARL: He has some plan.

MARION: Sit down for God's sake!

(He sits.)

MARION: There. Isn't that better? Now, what sort of plan?

CARL: I don't know—a plan. He means to hurt me in some way.

MARION: Why should he want to?

CARL: I don't know! He imagines I'm responsible for something.

MARION: Responsible for what?

CARL: I told you I don't know! He's crazy—that's the only way I can make any sense out of this. He's crazy since his wife died—maybe even before. Maybe he never even had a wife. He could be making it all up.

MARION: But why would he?

CARL: Why? Why? Because he's crazy, that's why!

MARION: You're getting paranoid.

CARL: He nearly rips off my arm, he throws me out of my own bedroom, he holds a knife at your throat—and you say I'm paranoid. Goddamn right I'm paranoid!

MARION: Steve was just playing with that knife. He meant it as a...symbol.

CARL: Symbol!

MARION: *(Overlapping)* He's teaching us a lesson. I don't know what it is yet, but I feel so calm, Carl. I feel so... strangely good today.

CARL: Did you do it last night, Marion? Is that why you feel so good?

MARION: You don't want to know. It'll just upset you.

CARL: Well, I hope to God it was at knife point. I hope you've left me that much of my dignity.

MARION: Your dignity is a very overrated quality. In fact, it's almost a defect in your character. It's turned you into a stuffed shirt.

CARL: Fine, fine. Now I'm a stuffed shirt. Thank you very much! It's not enough I've been up all night. It's not enough I cut myself with the damned screwdriver, trying to jimmy the basement door...

MARION: *(Maternally)* Let me see it. You did, didn't you? That's quite a nasty gash.

(She kisses it. For a moment, they look sheepishly at one another.)

CARL: Ah, Marion...Don't you love me anymore?

MARION: Of course I love you.

CARL: Then why is this happening to us? Why didn't you run away with me last night? Why can't I call the police?

MARION: *(Sternly)* You mustn't call the police, Carl. You must promise me—no police. He'd be furious. It would be very unpleasant.

CARL: I won't.

MARION: Promise?

CARL: I won't call them—I promise.

MARION: That's a relief. *(Slight pause)* Now look, Carl...we can get over this obstacle if we have patience to see it to the end. If we don't lose our heads. Submission, Carl. Submission is how we survive this violent interlude.

CARL: I am being submissive.

MARION: I know you are, sweetheart, and I love you for it. It's beautiful the way you're being so submissive. Beautiful and inspirational. Perhaps when this is all over, they'll nominate you for a major peace prize. Wouldn't that be nice?

CARL: Yes. But just between the two of us—I'm scared shitless.

MARION: Don't be. There's no reason. Everything is going to be all right. Listen to Momma.

CARL: But he said he didn't want to leave. Ever.

MARION: Steve was just talking through his hat. A lot of things were said in the heat of the moment. Now I'm sure when he gets tired of me and the house he'll move on. He'll find himself something better. He's terribly ambitious.

CARL: I've noticed.

MARION: So you know he's not going to be satisfied with this for too long. He'll be moving on soon—just you wait and see.

CARL: It's not easy for me.

MARION: Of course it isn't! It's very very hard. But just remember it's not easy for me either. Now I've got two men to pick up after, two men to cook and iron for, two men to please. It's exhausting!

(Pause)

CARL: Marion...?

MARION: Yes?

CARL: Would you?

MARION: Would I what?

CARL: Would you give it to me?

MARION: Oh, Carl...I was up half the night giving it to Steve. I'm so tired. And sore.

CARL: Please! I need a sign.

MARION: Well, we'll see. Maybe later.

CARL: Now, Marion! Give it to me now! Later, you may be busy with Steve.

MARION: Oh, all right! But it can't be upstairs. He's still asleep, and I don't want to wake him. He worked very hard last night.

CARL: Here! Right here!

MARION: *(Slightly shocked)* In the kitchen? In broad daylight? Suppose someone sees us?

CARL: I don't care. I want it.

MARION: *(Laughing)* You can be such a baby!

CARL: Come on, Marion—I can't wait much longer!

MARION: All right, all right. You're so impetuous.

(She opens her blouse and suckles him. He lays his head in her lap and makes little moans and gurgles of pleasure.)

MARION: There, there...such a baby.

(She hums a lullaby.)

(STEVE enters suddenly.)

STEVE: What's going on?

MARION: *(Happily)* Good morning! I'm just giving Carl a little suck. He's very depressed.

(STEVE bends down to speak to CARL.)

STEVE: How are you, Carl? How are you this morning?

(CARL is oblivious, sucking at MARION's breast.)

MARION: He didn't sleep a wink last night.

STEVE: That's too bad. He looks peaceful now.

MARION: Can I get you some breakfast?

STEVE: If there's any of that left, I'll have a tug myself.

MARION: *(Laughs)* Oh, Steve, don't make me laugh. It hurts!

STEVE: That's because the bugger still has his teeth. Want I should pull them out? It wouldn't be any trouble. Just yank out the little suckers, one by one.

MARION: That won't be necessary.

STEVE: It would give me the greatest pleasure.

MARION: That's your trouble. You're a hedonist. What you need is something to sink your teeth into.

(At that moment, CARL sinks his teeth into her.)

MARION: Ouch! Let me put it another way. You need to pick up the pieces of your life and move forward.

STEVE: That's just what I'm doing. I'm picking up the pieces and holding them to the light to see what went wrong. Your husband is one of the pieces.

MARION: *(Surprised)* Carl?

STEVE: Yes, Carl. A small piece to be sure, but as it turns out one of the more important ones.

MARION: I don't know what you mean.

STEVE: Don't you worry your pretty little head about it.

MARION: Do you really think it's pretty? Oh, look...he's asleep. Help me.

(They put CARL in a chair and gently lay his head on the table.)

MARION: He's heavy.

STEVE: From all that good living.

MARION: *(Seriously)* He's not a bad man, you know. Not as men go. A little weak, a little self-indulgent—but not vicious. Never vicious. And a good husband.

STEVE: I know. That's why I'm giving him every opportunity to redeem himself.

MARION: Redeem himself for what?

STEVE: Killing my wife.

MARION: Oh, I think you must be mistaken, Steve. Carl never killed anyone. I'd know—he can't keep a secret.

STEVE: I'm sorry to disappoint you, but I am in the possession of certain facts as the men from Scotland Yard love to say.

MARION: Can you tell me what they are?

STEVE: Not now. Carl must hear them first. He must have every chance to atone.

MARION: I don't know what to say. If my husband did do what you say, I'm sorry. But I can't help thinking you've made a mistake.

STEVE: No mistake, Marion. He's guilty. All that remains is the sentencing.

MARION: Sentencing? You're frightening me.

STEVE: Murder and retribution are frightening subjects.

MARION: I suppose so.

STEVE: I like Carl. I really do. It's unfortunate that circumstances have brought us to this. But I think there's a lesson to be learned.

MARION: So long as it doesn't hurt.

STEVE: You didn't worry about hurting him when you went to bed with me.

MARION: What does that have to do with anything? There are things between man and wife you can have no idea of.

STEVE: You're forgetting I was married.

MARION: From what you've said the relationship was morbidly overwrought.

STEVE: Carl killed my wife.

MARION: How can you be so sure of the facts? Perhaps there's a piece you haven't found yet. One that will exonerate him beyond all shadow of a doubt.

STEVE: I must remember to tell Carl of your unexpected devotion. *(Pause)* Marion? Would you kill for him?

MARION: Yes, I would.

STEVE: That's interesting. *(Pause)* Would you die for him?

MARION: *(Surprised)* You mean really die for him?

STEVE: Yes.

MARION: I don't know.

STEVE: Will you think about it please? I'd like to know.

MARION: Yes, I will, Steve.

STEVE: I need your answer by midnight Sunday.

MARION: All right.

STEVE: Now I'd like some breakfast.

MARION: *(Indicating* CARL*)* To see him sleeping there, you'd think he hadn't a care in the world.

STEVE: It's the sleep of the just. But don't let it fool you.

(Blackout)

ACT TWO

Scene 1

(The kitchen. Shortly after.)

(Lights up on STEVE *and* MARION.*)*

MARION: Why don't you tell me something about yourself? We know nothing about your life. Where you come from. Your family.

[Note: The bracketed lines in the following speeches were omitted from the Los Angeles Theater Center production.]

STEVE: I was born thirty-three years ago in a small, drab town at the mouth of the Delaware. [The town is called Shell Pile. It is noteworthy for the piles of bleached oyster shells lying on every available bit of open ground. The town flourished during the last century when the Delaware Bay oyster beds were among the richest in the world. Many fine homes were built there as well as restaurants, railway stations, dance halls, and pleasure parks. There is a photo of my great-grandmother parading in one such pleasure park in white hoopskirt, shirtwaist, and parasol. She is wearing a string of pearls. Whether they are genuine or dimestore, it's impossible to tell. Her husband was captain of an oyster boat working out of one of the dozen or so immense, low sheds that line the river, not only at Shell Pile but other towns with equally picturesque names like Bi-Valve, Money Island, and Fortesque. The towns continued to flourish into the 1950's when something called the Red Tide infiltrated the oyster beds and the prosperity abruptly ended. I was a sullen student and kept mostly to myself. My tenth grade history teacher assured my mother that I would be dead or in jail by my twenty-first birthday. My mother had piss-colored hair that looked as if it had been knotted into her scalp, like a doll's.]

MARION: That's fascinating, Steve.

STEVE: I was born thirty-three years ago in a working-class neighborhood of a large Eastern city. [The floor of the house was crooked. My toys would roll across it. The kitchen table was shimmed up with 45-cent paperback copies of Shakespeare. The house was on American Street. My mother used to wash not only our sidewalk but the bit of street in front of our house. She used to say the street was so clean you could eat off it. To my knowledge, nobody ever did. When I was ten, my mother sold out to a black family who broke the block. Before they could move in, the neighbors burned the house down. What the fire didn't finish, the fire department did. The city condemned the house and a contractor came and knocked it down with a wrecking ball. Then they put what was left on the back of a dump truck. Where the house stood, there is now a hole in the ground. A monument to racial equality and the Great Society on American Street.]

MARION: I don't understand...You didn't grow up on the Delaware?

STEVE: I may have. I've dreamt it in such detail. But I have dreamt other places just as clearly. Fifty years ago I was born in the Rumanian village of Lipova. [My parents had come from Germany after the War. They were farmers. They grew cotton, lentils, and sugar beets. They did well. They lived the happy, rural life. My father played the accordion. We danced in the kitchen. All of that. My mother wore her hair in long yellow braids. She looked like the Swiss Miss on the cocoa tin. Then the German army invaded Rumania and occupied Lipova. Being Germans, we did not suffer. Most of the non-Germans did suffer. Towards the end of the war, the German army left Lipova to fight the Russian army on the eastern border. The first thing the Rumanians did, after the last German soldier had left, was to hang all the collaborators. We had not collaborated, but that made no difference to the people of Lipova. We had prospered, and they had not. They hanged my father. And they shaved my mother's corn-colored hair. This was revenge and only natural. The German army was defeated by the Russian one. They came racing back in trucks, cars, motorcycles. They stopped in Lipova long enough to shoot the townspeople who had taken revenge on German sympathizers. My mother and I got into a truck and rode all night. We took some turnip jelly and potatoes and a bit of brown bread. Then we were in a train that was going to Hungary. At Budapest, the train crossed a bridge over the Danube. It was night. Searchlights swung back and forth over the black sky. Our boxcar was halfway across the bridge when the Russian planes came. They dropped incendiary bombs called Stalin Candles. We made ourselves very small in a corner of the boxcar and shut our eyes. Bombs blew up the part of the bridge we had just crossed, and the boxcars behind ours went screaming into the river, lit by Stalin Candles. There was a smell of apple blossoms which is characteristic of the chemical agent used in incendiaries.]

(Pause)

MARION: *(Not knowing what to make of all this)* Well, tell me about your wife.

STEVE: I had a wife, and then she died. I am correcting her death.

MARION: How can you, Steve? What's done is done.

STEVE: I've already started. Listen. A life for as long as it is singular, insular, is safe. It even has the possibility of immortality. But as soon as it comes into contact with another life, they ravel; they wrap around each other.

Sometimes the wrapping goes on for years, or a lifetime. Sometimes only a moment. I am unraveling all the strands that wrapped around my wife and choked her. And when I've unwrapped them all and severed them, she will live again.

MARION: That's an interesting theory. But of course you don't really believe it.

STEVE: I must or it won't happen.

(Pause)

MARION: Where were you before you came to live with us?

STEVE: You want to know whether I was in an institution.

(She reacts.)

STEVE: It's all right. It's only natural you should want to know. You do know I was insane for a while after her death? Yes, I remember telling you and Carl about it. It was during that time I conceived my theory of wrappings—which, I repeat, must be more than a theory if it is to work. It must be an obsession. *(Pause)* Being insane is not what most people think.

MARION: Isn't it?

STEVE: Not at all. Insanity is simply the mind out of phase. The brain is electrical, and sometimes it slips—or is pushed—out of sync. It continues to operate, but instead of the lights being on the outside, they're inside. When they give electroshock treatments, they're trying to jump the mind back into phase. But what they're really doing is lighting up the inside with incredible wattage. The whole interior grid seethes and snaps, and the lights which looked like ordinary 60-watt bulbs become floodlights. Which is not the desired effect.

MARION: It isn't?

STEVE: Oh, no. Because once the place is lit up completely, brilliantly, you never want to leave it. It's too beautiful.

Some never do leave it. *(Slight pause)* It's where the term "flashes of illumination" comes from.

MARION: It must be wonderful.

STEVE: It is. It's like Times Square, it's like Vegas, it's like an amusement park on a night when you were young, or a forest of blazing Christmas trees.

MARION: I'd like to see that.

STEVE: Maybe someday you will.

(Pause)

MARION: What about the future, Steve?

STEVE: The future is more complicated of course because new wrappings are constantly being made. That's why I prefer to operate strictly in the past.

MARION: Is that possible?

STEVE: No, in a sense I'm just kidding myself. But that's the fate of every philosopher and fanatic. Whoever commits himself to a single idea is just kidding himself.

(Pause)

MARION: Tell me another one of your lives—*(Laughs)* I almost said "lies"!

STEVE: They're not lies! They are possibilities that are not realized as strongly as the one we call our "life." And I'll tell you something even stranger. Each of those possibilities works itself out in time. By that I mean each has its past, present, and future. Each is going on at this very moment.

MARION: And do they carry us with them? Are we alive in all of them, simultaneously?

STEVE: Yes. Only paler so to speak. Those other lives are fainter.

MARION: But how is it we know nothing about them?

STEVE: We do! At night when we dream. Our dreams are a jumble of all our lives. That's why there are so many strangers in them, so many strange places. When you dream of making love to someone you've never seen before, that person is known to you—maybe even loved by you—in one of your other lives. Those cities that you think you visit only in your sleep—foreign cities many of them, with sinister streets and canals—they are your cities. All of them! In our dreams, our several lives cross. Psychologists have had to invent the subconscious to account for the magical quality of our mind that seems on one level to know everything—the world, all worlds and all times—instinctively. The wonderful truth is that we do know! Because our life as we call it (though by my theory it can hardly be called ours)—our life is composed of many strands, and each of these strands gets wrapped around others and so on and so on until before very long the whole planet is interlaced, like a vast circuit board. *(Slight pause)* It's all electrical.

MARION: It's mind-boggling!

STEVE: It's meant to be by whoever or whatever designed it.

MARION: Sometimes a picture pops into your head—from nowhere. For me, it's a place, a house not far from the ocean. With a spiral staircase. It's as strong as a memory, but I know I couldn't possibly have been there. And yet it's so familiar.

STEVE: We catch a glimpse, occasionally, of one of our other lives. Something happens and two strands fall across each other like bare wires. There's a momentary short-circuit, and we "see." *(Slight pause)* For the insane it's more or less permanent. They are living in every one of their lives simultaneously. The insulation...

MARION: The insulation?

STEVE: *(Shrugs)* It gets scraped away. The wires touch, and you're locked in. It's as if your TV were receiving and showing all stations at once. It's hypnotic. This is the true meaning of schizophrenia. And how else do we explain the whole parapsychological world? The psychic who tells the police she "saw" someone murdered is adept at slipping across borders. She travels through those strange countries, knows the dialects, the timetables, the rates of exchange...She is a witness to murder, or she is the murderer, or she is the murder victim.

MARION: And when we dream we are dying...what does it mean?

STEVE: I suspect that when we dream our own death, when we dream we're falling out a window, we are, somewhere. And the moment we wake, terrified and short of breath, we've died...somewhere. That's the only way to understand those dreams without a lot of mysticism. The psychologists made the subconscious into a kind of heaven and ask us to take it on faith. You can't touch it, taste it, smell it, see it, or measure it—just like heaven—but they insist we believe in it all the same.

MARION: And you really believe you can correct something that's already happened?

STEVE: We do it every night. It's what gives our dreams their strangeness. Not only the mixing but the correction of mistakes. We walk into a strange house and feel our necks prickling with terror. We go through a door to escape it and suddenly find ourselves on a train or a boat, in a garden or on a beach. We've jumped the banks of one life into another, which at that particular moment is less menacing. Why? To correct a mistake in judgment, or itinerary. *(Slight pause)* My wife is just across the border. I know because I dream her there. I hope to bring her back.

MARION: By killing Carl—or me?

STEVE: Your death would simply be a correction. She jumped this life in part because of Carl's violent, though unwitting, intervention. A second violent intervention may bring her back. If not, I'll just have to go looking for her.

MARION: Like Orpheus?

STEVE: Violently.   Violence   unlocks   every mystery—maybe even the ultimate one.

MARION: And what is the ultimate mystery?

STEVE: *(Shrugs)* Death, of course.

(Pause)

MARION: Well, this certainly has been stimulating. I don't remember when I've been so stimulated. Thank you, Steve.

STEVE: *(Preoccupied)* It's just possible that there is no death.

(Blackout)

Scene 2

(The living room. The next afternoon.)

(Lights up. Poster board is scattered over the floor. Several have been hand-lettered with lampoons such as "I Was Wrong," "Guilty As Charged," and "Killing Is Too Good For Me." MARION *and* CARL *are sitting on the floor. She is happily lettering a poster with marker.)*

MARION: I haven't done this since high school.

CARL: *(Sulking)* Well, I won't do it!

MARION: Don't be a spoiled-sport.

CARL: It's humiliating! Who does he think he is?

MARION: Where's the harm?

CARL: The harm is psychological.

MARION: I think it's fun.

CARL: It's not fun. It's autocriticism. They do it in Russia. It's one of the psychological weapons of the modern tyranny.

MARION: You should hear yourself, Carl. You sound just like Buckley. *(Slight pause)* Is mea culpa one word or two?

CARL: What are you writing? And what do you have to be sorry about?

MARION: You better do one. He'll be furious if you don't.

CARL: He's been awfully quiet this morning. Or should I say ominously?

MARION: He's in the basement, working. I heard him go down after breakfast.

CARL: What in the name of God is he doing down there?

MARION: I don't know. Carl, if you don't help me, I'll never finish in time to make dinner.

CARL: Remember how nice our Sundays were before he came?

MARION: Sure, it was only last week. He's been here exactly three days.

CARL: Seems like years. I can hardly remember what it felt like to live without fear. He's installed a reign of terror right under our very roof! Look at us, Marion. *(Indicating posters)* Look at this shit! What are we doing?

MARION: He promised to explain everything tonight.

CARL: I ought to sneak out of here right now while he's in the basement.

MARION: Why, have you done something wrong?

CARL: You tell me. He doesn't take me into his confidence.

MARION: Just because he brutalizes me now and then doesn't mean he tells me things. We'll just have to wait and see.

CARL: Has he said anything?

MARION: He said a great deal yesterday morning when you fell asleep at the table, but it was all theoretical.

CARL: What kind of theoretical?

MARION: He has some wild theory about schizophrenia and extrasensory perception...

CARL: What?

MARION: Oh, I don't know...It was all very confusing. I didn't understand a thing, except he believes his wife is still alive.

CARL: Yeah, where?

MARION: In some other life he is living, faintly, in some other place. It's all nonsense.

CARL: I think I'd be smart to leave right now.

MARION: Running away never solved anything.

CARL: What do I have to solve? Where's the problem?

MARION: He obviously believes you're guilty of some great crime.

CARL: That's ridiculous!

MARION: I know, darling, but he thinks you are. And in a couple of hours he'll confront you with it, and you can deny everything.

CARL: What good will it do? He's off his rocker.

MARION: He may still be able to listen to reason.

CARL: Have you ever tried to reason with a lunatic? That's why they have straitjackets and rubber rooms.

MARION: Shhh! Not so loud. He may not know he's a lunatic. The news might upset him.

CARL: If he doesn't know now, someone ought to tell him. It could change his attitude about a couple of things.

(Pause)

MARION: Do you have a gun, Carl?

CARL: You know I don't have a gun!

MARION: Husbands have their little secrets...

CARL: Well, I don't have one. *(Slight pause)* Why do you want to know?

MARION: Oh, no reason.

CARL: Do you think I need a gun?

MARION: No, whatever for?

CARL: You're the one who brought it up.

MARION: I was just making conversation.

CARL: Oh, it was a conversation piece. *(Slight pause)* This is the worst Sunday afternoon I ever spent.

MARION: The Sunday your brother came over and overfed the goldfish was worse. Remember how their little bellies blew up?

(Slight pause)

CARL: No, this is worse. I have a terrible feeling this is my last Sunday.

MARION: You are funny sometimes, Carl.

(A moody silence)

CARL: Do you think I should fight him?

MARION: A duel? Typewriters at twenty paces? No, I wouldn't. He's younger than you. And stronger. He has a very well-developed physique.

CARL: Maybe I could hit him over the head as he comes up the stairs.

MARION: You might miss.

CARL: Maybe I could tiptoe over to the basement door and lock it.

MARION: You could do that.

CARL: If I weren't so scared!

(He shudders violently.)

MARION: You're shaking like a leaf.

CARL: I'm not used to dealing with this sort of situation!

MARION: People like us rarely are.

CARL: Things like this aren't supposed to happen here! This isn't Harlem or downtown Beirut. This is a pleasant bedroom community starting in the upper 70's! We have Town Watch and the National Guard. We have burglar alarms!

MARION: We should never have let him in.

CARL: You let him in—not me!

MARION: I was just being sociable.

CARL: Things like this can't happen in New Jersey!

(He desperately seizes on this fallacious bit of wishful thinking.)

CARL: That's right, isn't it? Of course it is! We've got it all wrong, Marion.

MARION: Do we? I'm so glad.

CARL: This isn't downtown Beirut—this is New Jersey! Ha! We have nothing to worry about. This is a minor inconvenience—that's all. Nothing will happen. He'll probably shake me down for a couple hundred bucks and be on his way. He'll take the silver and the lithographs and be gone in the morning. Just you wait and see. He's had his fun.

MARION: You don't think you should try to escape?

CARL: Nah! It's reality shock, that's what it is. I've heard about guys like Steve. They go into a place with the idea of rubbing a few smug noses in reality. To wake us up. They're like the Mormons. You know we should thank him. We're forever in his debt. He's taught us terror. Terror is the big emotion of our time, and without him we might have lived and died without ever experiencing it. Terror is good for the bowels.

MARION: He's cut the phone wire.

CARL: What!

MARION: I tried to call my mother a little while ago, and the phone was dead.

CARL: *(Hopefully)* Maybe a line's down?

MARION: The wire was cut, Carl.

CARL: Which wire?

MARION: The one that goes from the wall to the phone.

CARL: Holy shit! What did he do that for?

MARION: *(Laughs)* For the good of our bowels?

(CARL *searches frantically for something he can use as a weapon.*)

CARL: There's nothing I can use as a weapon! That's the modern home for you! Everything safe, soft, and sanitized!

MARION: Try appeasement, Carl. It can be an effective short-term solution.

CARL: There's nothing I can even hit him with! No fire tongs, not even a goddamn ceremonial sword!

MARION: Why not break a window? You can call for help and use a piece of broken glass to defend yourself.

CARL: *(At the breaking point)* Because I couldn't stand to hear the glass break! It would be the end of me.

(STEVE *appears suddenly.*)

STEVE: Carl.

CARL: *(In a small, weak voice)* Yes, Steve?

STEVE: Will you come with me please?

CARL: *(Fearfully)* Where, Steve?

STEVE: To the cellar.

CARL: You mean the basement?

STEVE: The cellar. There's something I want to show you.

(Blackout)

Scene 3

(The basement workshop. A few minutes later.)

(Lights up. STEVE *is showing* CARL *what he has built. It is an electric chair, crudely fashioned from an old kitchen chair, light fixtures, hooded hair drier, leather belts, and wire.)*

STEVE: Well, what do you think of it?

CARL: What is it?

STEVE: Oh, come on, Carl...Use your imagination.

CARL: *(Incredulously)* It's...an electric chair?

STEVE: Of course it is. I admit it's makeshift, but it's in perfect working order.

CARL: For me?

STEVE: Perhaps. I did ask Marion if she wouldn't mind dying for you. She's not altogether unwilling. At least she promised to think about it.

CARL: *(Stupidly)* It's an electric chair.

STEVE: Yes, an electric chair.

CARL: What's it doing here?

STEVE: I built it.

CARL: But why?

STEVE: To help me make a correction.

CARL: What sort of correction?

STEVE: For the death of my wife. Didn't Marion tell you?

CARL: Tell me what?

STEVE: *(Angrily)* She should have told you.

CARL: Tell me what!

STEVE: That it was you who killed my wife. It was you who brought about the tragic events which brought me here. I've come to set things right.

CARL: I've never hurt anyone!

STEVE: That's just what Marion said. You know, I think she cares for you. It really surprised me. Of course, she doesn't believe any of this is happening. She thinks it's all a game.

CARL: I didn't kill your wife.

STEVE: Not knowingly. Not with malice. But you killed her just the same. You are responsible. I'll tell you frankly you are not the only one. I've got a list. You are one of seven persons. Six have already been dealt with.

CARL: I don't know what you think I did, but—

STEVE: You wrote the ad that killed her. That was nicely phrased, don't you think? The ad that killed her. Yes—it flows.

CARL: What ad?

STEVE: On the IUD. It ran in all the women's magazines last year. Don't you remember? Sure you do. It was a very good ad. My wife showed it to her doctor, and he fitted her with one. So we wouldn't have children. We wanted to put together a nest egg first.

CARL: I don't understand...

STEVE: Haven't you caught on yet? My wife died because some people thought they could shut themselves up in a box where the laws of accountability didn't apply. The doctor knew better, or should have. I cut off his finger—the one that inserted the device. That's a good name for it, don't you agree? You picture a small bomb deep in her innards—which is exactly what it turned out to be. It was the doctor's idea to add you to my list. He said why stop at him? Why not go after the people who wrote the ad?

CARL: That's insane!

STEVE: *(Ignoring him)* I cut the throat of the president of the IUD company without so much as an introduction. So you see I have a sense of justice. To each according to his crime. Because yours is more willful ignorance than anything, I have taken pains to help you atone.

CARL: *(Hotly)* You can't hold me responsible for that product! No court in the world would.

STEVE: This court does.

CARL: What court?

STEVE: The one that's now in session. Oh, don't worry... It will be very informal. It remains only for me to sentence you.

CARL: You can't do this!

STEVE: Of course I can. Crazy people can do anything.

CARL: I refuse to be judged by a crazy person.

STEVE: Historically, justice has always been in the hands of the insane. Anyway, you don't have any choice. Sit down, please.

CARL: Where?

STEVE: In the chair. Get the feel of it.

CARL: I don't want to.

STEVE: Now!

(He pushes CARL into the chair.)

STEVE: It fits. Don't be so nervous. I won't throw the switch. Not yet. This is your sentencing, not your execution. Besides, we haven't heard from Marion. She may choose to take your place. It's possible. Is she a religious woman? *(No response)* Well, we'll see.

CARL: Please. I don't want to die.

STEVE: Is life that important to you?

CARL: Yes!

STEVE: That surprises me. You seem like such a superficial person to me. Merely floating above the surface of life, like a Hovercraft.

CARL: I'm only thirty-six for Christ's sake!

STEVE: Christ is known for many things, but longevity isn't one of them. So I wouldn't bother invoking His name.

CARL: I didn't know I was hurting anybody!

STEVE: Ignorance is no excuse in the eyes of the law. It's bliss but no excuse. You are guilty of complicity in the death of my wife. Do you have anything to say before this court passes sentence?

CARL: *(Attempting to rise)* I do not recognize the authority of this court.

(STEVE pushes him roughly back into the chair.)

STEVE: Sit down! Our authority cannot be challenged.

CARL: *(Softly)* Take Marion.

STEVE: What's that?

CARL: Marion. Kill her. I don't owe her anything. Not after what she's done to me.

STEVE: What has she done to you?

CARL: Humiliated me!

STEVE: How?

CARL: By going to bed with you!

STEVE: Don't be a fool. Women can't help themselves in the presence of diabolical power. It attracts them. It's a law of nature on a par with gravitation. Marion doesn't love me.

CARL: She let you screw her! She's dirty. I never want to see her again. You can have her, the house—everything—just let me go. I'll never come back. And I won't tell anyone—I swear it.

STEVE: *(Disgusted)* Stop whimpering! Have some dignity, man! Life isn't worth losing your dignity.

CARL: I don't want to die.

STEVE: This is getting us nowhere. And so without further ado, I sentence you to death, sentence to be carried out at 12 midnight. Unless someone is willing to sit in for you. And may your soul rest in peace, which is damned generous of me under the circumstances.

CARL: Let me choose.

STEVE: Choose what? Your mode of execution? *(Indicating the electric chair)* Would you have all this go to waste?

CARL: Let me choose who is to die—me or Marion.

STEVE: Would you really want such power? The power of life and death? You'd be on the front lines, so to speak, instead of safe in the rear, writing a war department handbook. Do you get the analogy? You're a writer—you don't do the dirty work.

CARL: You've taken the power of life and death in your hands.

STEVE: That's different. I'm the judge. I have moral authority behind me.

CARL: Who gave it to you?

STEVE: I took it. Because in the tangle of modern jurisprudence, it was lost. Have you ever read any of the old Viking sagas? There is a simple moral principle in all of them. If someone close to you — your kin—is murdered, it is your legal and sacred right to ask for—take—a life of equal value. A life of equal value! Not only an eye for an eye...a wife for a wife. Which is why I asked yours if she were willing to die in your place.

CARL: There's been a thousand years of moral progress since the Vikings!

STEVE: Progress when some animal can pistolfuck a woman, pull the trigger, and get parole in seven years? There has been no progress, Carl. Our legal system swings crazily back and forth between barbarism and sentimentality, but morality hasn't changed one bit.

CARL: I write ads! I am not a murderer.

STEVE: But you are. Don't you understand? *(Slight pause)* Not that there aren't degrees of guilt...Remember the fingerless gynecologist?

(He makes a truncated obscene gesture and laughs.)

STEVE: The president of the IUD company died with his sins unforgiven. You, Carl, I am giving the chance of dying with self-knowledge. This is the essence of tragedy. Anything else would be melodramatic.

CARL: I want no part of your tragedy.

STEVE: But you're its author.

(CARL holds up his two index fingers.)

CARL: Take these—I type with them. Why can't you be satisfied with them? Why am I on trial for my life?

STEVE: Because of the seven persons implicated in the crime, you are the one with the words. You are the only one who I imagined would be able to articulate his guilt.

CARL: But I'm not guilty!

(Pause)

STEVE: Yes, you have been a disappointment. But all the same, I couldn't possibly let you go on living. You might tell someone. Listen, Carl...We are alive for such a short time anyway, isn't it better to die well now and take your chances in paradise?

CARL: I don't believe in paradise.

STEVE: Oh? Well, there's still the peace of the grave. Now that you know you helped kill an innocent woman, you won't be able to live with yourself.

CARL: Yes, I will.

STEVE: That's the wrong thing to say. I'd cut you in two with your own Skilsaw if I thought you were incapable of making an Act of Contrition.

CARL: Marion will satisfy your Viking sense of justice!

STEVE: But I'm worried about you, Carl.

CARL: Don't be.

STEVE: I'm worried that you couldn't survive with two murders on your conscience.

CARL: I want to live.

STEVE: At any price?

CARL: Any price.

STEVE: I can't help thinking you're making a mistake. Why not finish it right now? You see the switch there on the arm of the chair? That one, yes. All you have to do is flip it. You'll feel better almost immediately.

CARL: *(No longer able to plead)* Take Marion.

(Pause)

STEVE: Well, I'll think about it—I surely will. I'll let you know. *(Slight pause)* You can get up now.

(CARL drops onto the floor and kisses STEVE's foot.)

STEVE: *(Kicking him)* Don't do that! It's not dignified.

CARL: Thank you.

(STEVE begins to exit.)

STEVE: I'm going upstairs and think about our conversation. You think, too.

CARL: Do I have to stay here?

STEVE: I'm afraid so. I think it would be best if I locked you in. It'll help you to think.

CARL: *(Like a frightened child)* Will you leave the light on?

STEVE: For a while.

CARL: Thank you.

STEVE: Maybe Marion will come and see you later.

CARL: Marion?

STEVE: Yes, and Carl...don't be afraid to kill to stay alive.

(STEVE *tosses him a knife and exits. The lights dim out—all but the single light bulb hanging over the electric chair.)*

(Blackout)

Scene 4

(The living room. Shortly after.)

(Lights up. STEVE *and* MARION *are talking.)*

STEVE: The trouble with Carl is he has no moral grandeur.

MARION: I'm sorry I ever let you touch me.

STEVE: Does that mean you've decided to die in his place?

MARION: You're not serious?

STEVE: It's nearly time.

MARION: Time for what?

STEVE: *(Angrily)* Haven't either of you been paying attention! In a little while someone must die to correct my wife's death.

MARION: You're joking!

STEVE: What do you think this has all been? A game?

MARION: I thought you wanted to scare us—

STEVE: To death. Come on now, Marion...are you willing? In all fairness I must say that Carl has done his best to nominate you for the honor.

MARION: Oh, he did?

STEVE: He was very eloquent. In fact, he nearly convinced me.

MARION: *(Incredulously)* He really told you to kill me?

STEVE: Really and truly. Does that surprise you? It shouldn't. It takes an insane amount of courage to make the ultimate sacrifice, and I'm afraid Carl is perfectly sane.

MARION: The bastard!

STEVE: I wouldn't be too hard on him. If it were an easy thing to do, we would have no need of Christ.

MARION: I was seriously considering doing it, but now... he can forget it.

STEVE: Were you really, or are you just saying it to impress me?

MARION: No, I really was.

(STEVE *makes a few notes in his notebook.*)

STEVE: That's very interesting. I want to make a note of that.

MARION: Why?

STEVE: Don't be so suspicious. We're participating—all three of us—in a unique experiment. An experiment in home justice. It's only natural I should want a record of the highlights.

MARION: I hate you.

STEVE: Enough to kill me?

MARION: *(Coldly)* Yes.

STEVE: Good. You may get the chance later on.

MARION: What do you mean?

STEVE: *(Ignoring her)* Carl, on the other hand, seems to have lost all his hatred. Why do you think that is? He kissed my foot just now. Strange.

MARION: I hate you both.

STEVE: It's almost as if he looked on me as his savior... someone with infinite power over his life.

MARION: You're enjoying this, aren't you?

STEVE: Suffering has its compensations.

MARION: Why don't you leave now while you still can?

STEVE: I've made myself responsible and will see you through to the bitter end. Besides, I've come to believe that I have no life outside this house.

MARION: This is not your house! This is my house and Carl's. Go away!

STEVE: It's too late. I'm like a mine waiting just below the water for a passing ship. There's no going back.

MARION: Please leave us alone. There's a chance, if you go right now, Carl and me can still put our life back together.

(Pause)

STEVE: I want you to kill him.

MARION: *(Horrified)* What!

STEVE: I've locked him in the cellar. I have given him the reasons and the means to kill himself. I have also given him the opportunity of making a substitution. You.

(She reacts.)

STEVE: Don't interrupt. I have given you the chance to save him, which you have refused. I want you to kill him for me, if he doesn't do it himself.

(He gives her a knife.)

STEVE: Use it on Carl.

MARION: *(Dropping the knife in horror)* No!

STEVE: You must be ready to defend yourself.

MARION: What do you mean "defend myself"?

STEVE: Carl also has a knife. I gave it to him when I was in the cellar just now. In a little while I'm going to unlock the door. He'll be coming for you, Marion.

(He puts the knife back into her hands, and this time she does not drop it.)

MARION: He wouldn't hurt me.

STEVE: He hates you for sleeping with me. He hates you for not running away with him. He hates you because you've seen his humiliation.

MARION: Did you plan all this?

STEVE: Every last detail. And you and Carl obeyed every prompting, every direction. You have given the performance of your lives.

MARION: Why didn't you just murder us in our beds?

STEVE: I wanted you to know the anguish I have known. I wanted you, Marion, to suffer a little of what my wife suffered before she died from Carl's prize-winning words!

MARION: I should have called the police.

STEVE: And now it's too late. The phone is dead. The doors locked. The windows nailed shut. And in a very few minutes, all the lights will go out, thanks to a small electrical device I've installed in the breaker box. It should be a lot of fun, roaming through the dark with knives in our hands. Oh, yes...

(He shows her his knife.)

STEVE: I have a knife, too. Someone is going to die tonight, but not even I know who.

(She rushes suddenly at him with the knife.)

MARION: I'll kill you, you fucker!

(He disarms her easily.)

STEVE: It won't be so easy for me to do that in the dark. You can sneak up on me in the dark and cut my throat. Of course, it may be Carl's throat. You won't know until the lights come back on. Which they will at exactly 12:15.

(She falls, sobbing, onto the floor.)

STEVE: I liked you better before.

MARION: Kill Carl. Kill Carl and leave me alone. I'll do anything you want.

STEVE: Carl was right. You are getting fat. Now here's the situation. Carl is locked in the cellar with his knife. He knows that his one chance is to kill you or me. We agree that it will probably be you. You have a knife and realize that you must use it on me or Carl to stay alive. I, if I wish to stay alive, must kill one or both of you first. There is no escape from the house. Your nearest neighbor is down the road and out of earshot. So much for the insular lifestyle.

(He looks at his watch.)

STEVE: One minute to twelve. Carl has sixty seconds to execute his sentence and save us—we'll know if the lights flicker. You have your knife, I have mine. When the lights go out, I will walk quickly to the cellar door and unlock it. If Carl is waiting at the top of the steps, there is a chance he can get to me. If he's not, I'll go and hide somewhere in the house till I get a chance at him. You can hide under a bed or go down the cellar, as you choose.

(Looks at his watch.)

STEVE: Fifteen seconds. Looks like Carl has had a failure of nerve. Or perhaps he's already coming quietly up the stairs...

MARION: What happens if no one is dead when the lights come on?

STEVE: We do it again.

MARION: I couldn't go through it again.

(He takes her hand.)

STEVE: Then let's all go down to the cellar.

(Blackout)

Scene 5

(The living room. One year later.)

(Lights up. CARL is showing STEVE a photo album. They are on the sofa. STEVE is catatonic, and smiling.)

CARL: Here you are in the electric chair. Here you are being carried by the ambulance men up the stairs. That's you under the blanket.

(He is enjoying himself as he terrorizes STEVE.)

CARL: We thought you were dead. You were so stiff and your eyes just staring into space. We thought you had to be dead. You took a terrible jolt. Here you are in the back of the ambulance. I'll remember that night as long as I live. I really will. And here you are in the emergency room. That's the trauma bay. They say you'll never be able to walk or talk again. You burned out such important parts of your brain.

(He takes a pin and sticks it into STEVE's leg. He doesn't flinch.)

CARL: That's how they test for paralysis. Interesting, don't you think? Now here's my favorite shot...Your homecoming day! Didn't the house look nice? Remember the crepe paper streamers and the cake? The first day of spring, too. Such a perfect day to come home! The crocuses were out. The sun was so warm. I'm glad it didn't rain. The rain might have made your nose itch, and you wouldn't have been able to scratch. And here you are on the toilet. In your own bathroom. You must always think of the guestroom as yours. You are our permanent guest, and we'll always take care of you. After all you've suffered ...Can you understand what I'm saying? I hope so. *(Pause)* It's nice having you to look after. I suppose

Marion and I should have had children...But now we have you instead. Can I get you anything? A drink of water? Some Kool-Aid? Soon I'll bring you something nice to eat. Mashed bananas? Tapioca pudding? Jello? We'll see. It'll be nice. And tonight there's a special television event on. I don't know what it is, but I'm sure it'll be terrific. They've been talking about it all day. And then you'll sleep. *(Pause)* What do you dream about, Steve? I'd love to know. Maybe you don't dream at all. No one seems to know. Science is still in the dark when it comes to the human mind. Especially a mind like yours that's all shut up in a dark box. It must be awful. Does it scare you, Steve? Are you scared all the time? Or just at night? Or maybe not at all...No one seems to know. *(Pause)* I'll bet you never thought you'd end up like this. A vegetable. A piece of New Jersey asparagus! Ha! Ha! It's all the fault of your strange obsession with justice. You should have buried your grief instead of dwelling on it. Don't dwell on things, my mother used to say. She was right. *(Pause)* What are you thinking about in that shut-up mind of yours?

(He shines a light in STEVE's *face.)*

CARL: I'll bet you're dwelling on things. I bet that's just what you're doing! Or are you dreaming of her...? If only I could reach you, bring you out of yourself. Oh, well. Maybe this summer we can go on a trip to the islands. Remember the islands, Steve? The four-star hotel with the view of the ocean? The sailboats? Maybe we can go. That would be wonderful! It's so serene there. We can't have too much serenity in our lives. I know it would do you a world of good. If you could only get a little hand/eye coordination going... some gross motor skills. You could have a hobby. You could fingerpaint or pick your nose. You could lick envelopes and earn some pocket money. You could become a useful member of society again. But here you sit like a lump, smiling like an idiot! It's infuriating the way you're always smiling! What do you have to smile about anyway? Are you being cynical? Are you making fun of me? I wish I knew. *(Pause)* Do you know, Steve, sometimes I'd like to bash your stupid face in. But only for a moment. The feeling passes. Because really we have to thank you for giving new meaning to our lives.

(MARION *enters. She wears a well-tailored suit and carries a briefcase.*)

MARION: Carl, I'm home.

CARL: *(Kissing her cheek)* Hello, dear, how was work?

MARION: Fine. I orchestrated another bloody corporate takeover. How was your day?

CARL: Quiet. I was just showing Steve the family album.

MARION: Great. How are you today, Steve?

(She slaps his back and shouts at him as if he were deaf.)

CARL: He's had a good day. He held his spoon.

MARION: Held his spoon? My, my—isn't that wonderful!

CARL: Of course he only held it for a second, and I doubt he'll ever be able to use one—I mean, to eat with—but he held it.

MARION: He's coming along—that's the important thing. *(To* STEVE*)* You're coming along! You're improving!

*(*CARL *shows* MARION *a photo.)*

CARL: Remember this one?

MARION: Sure! Steve's first time in the hot tub. Look at him smile.

CARL: He's always smiling.

MARION: And there's the mermaid I gave him. See the mermaid, Steve? Half girl, half fish. She's rubber, of course, but a rubber mermaid is just as good as a real one for a man lacking even the most rudimentary social skills. *(To* CARL*)* Did you wash my black turtleneck?

CARL: You're not going out again tonight?

MARION: There's a Neo-Nazi living over on Fourth Street.

CARL: But that makes every night this week! You'll wear yourself out.

MARION: There's a lot of wrongs to right, a lot of injustice flourishing under the protection of free speech.

CARL: I know, dear, but you're looking so tired lately. Can't somebody else deal with the Neo-Nazi? Just this once?

MARION: Sorry. I can't shirk my responsibilities. Steve taught me that. Didn't you, Steve? *(To* CARL*)* Isn't it funny the way he's always smiling?

CARL: It gives me the creeps.

MARION: Well, Steve has turned inward now. His work on the outside is finished. It's up to us to carry on.

CARL: But, Marion...I had plans for tonight! *(Seductively)* A quiet dinner—just the two of us...music, a bucket of champagne. I rented a porno flick. And I've bought you a new nightie. It's hot, Marion—it leaves nothing to the imagination. It's trimmed with real muskrat. I ordered it by mail, Marion—it's a mail-order nightie!

MARION: I'll try and be home early.

CARL: That's what you say every night! And it's always the same thing! You crawl in at two in the morning, stinking of beer, and all you can talk about is your latest assassination! You're becoming a bore, Marion, a four-star bore! I'm tired of playing nursemaid to this thing in our living room!

MARION: Shhh! He may still be able to hear.

CARL: He can't hear a thing in that rockbound cranium. I'm sorry, Marion, but for the past four months my life has revolved around Steve! I wash him, shave him, dress him, feed him, and change him. At least you get to go out at night. You meet exciting people.

MARION: All the exciting people I meet end up dead.

CARL: But you talk to them before you kill them, cite their crimes against humanity...sentence them to death. I'll bet they have all sorts of interesting things to say while they beg for their lives. I talk to a vegetable all day! I call up all the emergency hot lines just to have a conversation. Today, I called the Sexual Abuse Hotline and pretended to be a woman. It's not normal!

MARION: What do you want me to do? Turn my back on my fellow man?

CARL: Screw your fellow man! I want you to pay some attention to me!

MARION: The old life is dead. It died the night we nearly did. I had a vision while I was stumbling about in the dark. I saw my life for what it was. Mean, shallow, trivial. We did nothing but store up treasures, Carl. We neglected the unfortunates of this earth and bought lithographs and duck stamps instead. Until that "vegetable" as you call him came into our home, I never knew what it meant to be a human being. Remember the Jews of the Holocaust. Remember Dachau, remember Auschwitz, remember Birkenau, remember the Warsaw Ghetto—

CARL: Remember the Alamo.

MARION: Humanity is locked in a titanic struggle for survival, and we worried about regrouting the bathroom tile. We worried about our IRA account when the Irish Republican Army was starving in H-Block! We worried about our waist lines while the Africans died of hunger.

CARL: I liked you better when you didn't have a social conscience.

MARION: I was a parasite.

CARL: But you were fun. We did things as a family.

MARION: Would you like to come with me tonight? There's still time to get a sitter.

CARL: And watch you wire some poor fuck's balls to a car battery?

MARION: You can shine the flashlight in his face.

CARL: No thanks. I'd rather watch the Big Movie.

MARION: Suit yourself. Look, I promise—I'll do it quick tonight. No slow torture. And I'll come straight home instead of stopping off for a drink. Watch the Big Movie, put Steve to bed, and by the time you finish your shower, I'll be home and ready to slip into that new nightie.

CARL: Could you tie me to the bed?

MARION: Sure, I can tie you to the bed. It'll be just like old times. Almost.

(Pause)

CARL: I'm sorry for the way I acted just now. I was frivolous.

MARION: No problem. It's just your nature. *(Pause)* Are you proud of me, Carl?

CARL: I'm very proud of you. *(Pause)* Shall I pack you a sandwich?

MARION: Meatloaf?

CARL: *(Nodding)* Meatloaf.

(They embrace a moment, happily.)

MARION: Things are going to be all right. I can feel it. We're onto something here.

CARL: The Ultimate Secret?

MARION: Maybe. And we owe it all to Steve.

CARL: Good old Steve.

MARION: He's a saint, that's what I think.

CARL: We won't get the full benefit until he's dead.

MARION: I've ordered a modest stone. It'll be delivered sometime next month.

CARL: I don't know where you find the time.

MARION: It's easy once you get your priorities straight.

(CARL *puts a brown bag over* STEVE's *head.*)

MARION: What are you doing?

CARL: Sensory deprivation experiments. I'm trying to wipe that smile off his face.

MARION: I've been collecting some interesting data on that subject myself. We should pool our efforts.

(CARL *removes the bag.*)

CARL: *(Eagerly)* You mean collaborate?

MARION: Why not? We might publish a monograph.

CARL: Steve has really brought us together.

MARION: Yes. *(Pause)* There's just one thing I don't understand.

CARL: What's that?

MARION: What you could possibly have said to get him into the chair that night.

CARL: *(Surprised)* What I said? I thought it was something you said.

(Pause)

(MARION *begins to laugh, then* CARL. *Together, they laugh with increasing abandon until, suddenly, they are joined by* STEVE, *whose demonic laughter drowns theirs as the lights fade.*)

(Blackout)

WILD AND CRAZY PLAYS:

full length, contemporary, & American

BATTERY
Daniel Therriault
$4.95

BEIRUT
Alan Bowne
$4.95

HIGHEST STANDARD OF LIVING
Keith Reddin
$4.95

HOUSE OF CORRECTION
Norman Lock
$4.95

NATIVE SPEECH
Eric Overmyer
$4.95

ON THE VERGE
Eric Overmyer
$4.95

WALK THE DOG WILLIE
Robert Auletta
$4.95

Shipping is $2.00 for the first book ordered, and 25 cents for each book thereafter.

ANTI-NATURALISM

A manifesto against kitchen sink and trailer park plays

$12.95

BAL
Richard Nelson

HARM'S WAY
Mac Wellman

HIGHEST STANDARD OF LIVING
Keith Reddin

ON THE VERGE
Eric Overmyer

RECKLESS
Craig Lucas

THE WHITE DEATH
Daniel Therriault

THE GREAT THEATERS OF AMERICA

PLAYS FROM CIRCLE REP
$12.95

ENSEMBLE STUDIO MARATHON '84
$4.95

SHORT PIECES FROM THE NEW DRAMATISTS
$4.95

PLAYS FROM THE NEW YORK SHAKESPEARE FESTIVAL
$12.95

HIGH ENERGY MUSICALS FROM THE OMAHA MAGIC THEATER
$9.95

PLAYS FROM PLAYWRIGHTS HORIZONS
$12.95

Shipping is $2.00 for the first book ordered, and 25 cents for each book thereafter.

ONE ACTS, SHORT PIECES and MONOLOGS

BIG TIME and AFTER SCHOOL SPECIAL
Keith Reddin
$4.95

FUTZ and WHO DO YOU WANT, PEIRE VIDAL?
Rochelle Owens
$4.95

ONE ACTS AND MONOLOGUES FOR WOMEN
Ludmilla Bollow
$4.95

ORCHARDS
$4.95

ORGASMO ADULTO ESCAPES FROM THE ZOO
Dario Fo and Franca Rame
American adaptation by Estelle Parsons
$4.95

PLAYS BY JOE PINTAURO
$9.95

SHORT PIECES FROM THE NEW DRAMATISTS
$4.95

TRANSIENTS WELCOME
Rosalyn Drexler
$4.95

Shipping is $2.00 for the first book ordered, and 25 cents
for each book thereafter.